Clean Food

C R U S H

PUMPKIN LOVE

65 Clean, Simple, and Delicious Pumpkin Recipes!

Rachel Maser

CleanFoodCrush.com

Clean Food

CRUSH

Rachel Maser

Copyright © 2015 Rachel Maser

All rights reserved.

ISBN: 0692502831

ISBN-13: 978-0692502839

DEDICATION

To my 4 children for being my official taste testers, and main source of sweetness.

TABLE OF CONTENTS

Clean Food

CRUSH

Rachel Maser has become the leading go-to for clean, quick, inexpensive, and healthy eating for busy Moms with busy families. Rachel began her own journey in 2013 when some of her fitness friends started asking for her delicious and quick, but clean and healthy recipes.

Rachel started posting her recipes for her friends on social media, and they quickly went viral. Rachel now has hundreds of thousands of online followers and just as many friends, who all look to her for her innovative and nutritious FUN food ideas.

Rachel has turned her recipes and ideas into multiple cookbooks containing hundreds of quick, easy, and clean recipes. She has created several groups & programs where she personally coaches people to become a little more healthy.

Rachel has also authored 30 Days of Clean and Easy Recipes which has been widely recognized as the must have beginner clean food cookbook for busy families across the globe.

Rachel is extremely passionate about teaching the concept of real food tasting great and being simple to prepare. Her creations are always about real, whole foods. She enjoys teaching cooking classes, meal prep courses, and in-home cooking parties. She envisions these classes spanning the globe over the next several years.

Her TRUE passion lies within pointing others down this path of simplicity ease for homemade food, and then watching their lives evolve and light up!

Rachel has seen how real nutrition changes lives, and how it changes families. She knows the need families have to gain access to fun, easy, inexpensive, real food ideas that are doable for the lifestyle of busy women.

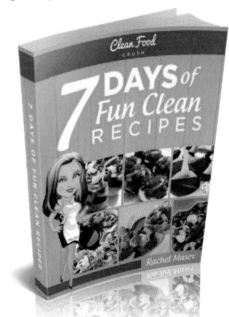

Rachel's most valued role is a busy Mom to 4 kids under the age of 12.

CleanFoodCrush (CFC) is Rachel's 5th child, one she gives to the world as a gift of Health, Hope, & Love.

Rachel's Free eCookbook 7 Days of Fun Clean Recipes has been downloaded over 25,000 times by families in all 50 states and many countries around the world.

Download Your Free Copy Today: http://CleanFoodCrush.com/7days

Hi there!

What you're about to read may be a little bit shocking. Especially, after everything you just read...

I share for that EXACT reason.

It's the complete truth.

This is not to embarrass my family, it's meant to show how far we've come.

It does not make me a victim to share my story, it helps me rise above it.

I have felt a VERY strong push to tell this story to others, because it gives us all the power to realize that CHANGE IS POSSIBLE, and what we tell ourselves TODAY is what really matters - NOT WHERE we were yesterday!

MY STORY. My REAL story.

Not the shiny, pretty clean food, biceps, healthy kids, "perfect" life story...but, me.

When I was 16, I moved out on my own. I grew-up in the very small town of Moab, Utah. It probably surprises you that I smoked cigarettes heavily from the age 16-20. I became involved with drugs. I liked to smoke weed occasionally, but I really preferred crystal meth.

For 2 years I lived for it. I loved the high I could get, then I would crash HARD. Losing all energy, and staying in bed for a few days at a time.

My health and ambition COMPLETELY sucked. I thought that I was a lost cause. I didn't know what to do most days. Something inside me said to change, so I did. Nothing big happened. I just realized that it was probably going to kill me.. I stopped using drugs completely. I just made myself stop.

When I became pregnant with my first baby at 20, I stopped smoking cigarettes. Just like that. I had always wanted to be a mother, so I told myself to just stop.

Throughout my 20's I gave birth to 4 (beautiful) children, didn't work-out very often, and became addicted to something else.

SUGAR.

I loved to bake, and make treats. I felt like CRAP. I just thought, "Well, I'm getting older, this is what happens." I also thought I was being such a "good" mom by making them enormous amounts of cookies and cupcakes, just about every day.

Something happened again...I faced the truth that was inside me all along...I realized that I absolutely knew better.

Just like nicotine...the sugar was VERY addictive, but it was still a choice. I was making excuses. I was taking the easy way out every day. The thing is, that it was NOT really that easy!

I was not happy with my energy or physical appearance. I was suffering because of my daily choices. So, I changed.

Just like that.

I began intensively researching health, and fitness. Making better lifestyle choices that felt right & good.

This is when my life completely opened up, and became a lot more FUN & meaningful. Those little choices we CAN make each day... they set us free.

Does not mean I'm "perfect" about the clean eating now, but my life HAS changed drastically. I understand that everything I put into my body will affect my mood, energy, health, and ultimately my quality of life.

It is a choice. A choice we all CAN make. It does not matter where we are from, what we have done in our past, or how far "gone" we think we are. None of that has ever mattered.

Just a choice we can make TODAY. It's never too late.

The truth can set us free, and inspire others.

Wishing you a lifetime of health & happiness on your own journey,

 Rachel

What is Clean Eating?

Clean Eating is the habit of avoiding processed and refined food.

- Eat only whole foods,
- Avoid processed foods.
- Eliminate refined sugars.
- Eat five or six smaller meals per day.
- Cook your own meals at home.

CLEAN EATING is a huge trend right now.

It is the "IN" thing to do for VERY good reasons!

There is not a definitive "guide" as to what is actually "clean" and what is not.

It's up to the individual to decide what it truly means to them.

It is now "cool" to find ways to incorporate more fruits & vegetables into our families diets!

People are seeking out fun ideas to rely as little as possible on packaged & processed foods.

Where did it come from?

The truth is, it's always been around! Clean Eating means to eat REAL food.

You know... the stuff our bodies need!

Why is it important?

Proper diet and nutrition affects every single aspect of our lives.

Our health & happiness are a direct result of our diet & lifestyle.

What are the benefits?

I receive messages daily, detailing how this CLEAN EATING has helped families improve their health & happiness in every way possible.

I'm grateful to be a part of this!

This movement is helping people think about what they are eating & encouraging to eat for nutritional value & fuel, rather than entertainment.

It's about making better personal choices each day...

What about food prepping?

When I first started food prepping it took me 3-4 hours because I honestly did not know where to even start!

Now it just takes me about an hour-2 at most.

Unless of course I am recipe experimenting, or just enjoying my kitchen time, then it can take me a little longer!

Yes, food prepping is just like working out or cleaning the house:

I don't always want to do it, but I always feel SO MUCH better when I do!

I hope this guide helps you and shortens your "learning curve".

{ One - Pumpkin Treats }

"Bittersweet October. The mellow, messy, leaf-kicking, perfect pause between the opposing miseries of summer and winter."

~ Carol Bishop Hipps ~

SIMPLE ROASTED PUMPKIN SEEDS

Ingredients:

▸ 1 ½ cups raw whole pumpkin seeds

▸ 1 tablespoon extra virgin olive oil or avocado oil

▸ sea salt to taste

Directions:

1. Preheat oven to 300°F

2. Toss seeds in a bowl with the oil and salt. Spread the seeds in a single layer on a baking sheet and bake for about 45 minutes or until golden brown; stir occasionally.

> Don't forget about the pumpkin seeds. These edible treasures are full of magnesium that help protect nerve and muscle function.

Gourmet Pumpkin Seeds

Ingredients:

- The Pumpkin seeds from one whole medium pumpkin, about 6-8 cups
- 2 tablespoons Avocado Oil or Olive Oil
- Sea salt to taste

OPTIONS - use any of these or none :)
- Garlic Salt
- Cumin and Chili Powder
- Curry
- Curry and Cayenne

Directions:

1. Scoop out the seeds and pulp from a pumpkin. Separate the pulp from the seeds, discarding the pulp.

2. Rinse the seeds under cold running water, removing any remaining pumpkin material.

3. Place seeds, a small amount at a time, into paper towels to dry.

4. Spread onto a large baking sheet and allow to finish air-drying for an hour or so.

5. Once seeds are dry, toss them with the oil to coat well and sprinkle with salt.

6. Spread into a thin layer on baking sheet. Place in oven for 45 minutes at 300°F, or until golden brown, stirring every few minutes to prevent burning.

7. Remove from the oven and allow to cool before serving.

Tangy Roasted Pumpkin Seeds

Ingredients:

- 2 cups freshly harvested pumpkin seeds
- 1 teaspoon Worcestershire sauce
- 1 1/2 tablespoons extra virgin olive oil or unrefined coconut oil
- 1 1/4 teaspoons sea salt

Directions:

1. Preheat oven to 300°F

2. Thoroughly rinse seeds and pick out stray bits of pumpkin guts.

3. Pour seeds on a flat cookie sheet, with sides.

4. Combine Worcestershire sauce and oil.

5. Pour Worcestershire sauce combination over seeds and stir to distribute evenly.

6. Evenly sprinkle salt over seeds.

7. Bake for about 45 minutes, or until golden brown, stirring every few minutes to prevent burning.

8. Let cool and enjoy your treat!

9. Store in airtight container.

Pumpkin Protein Bliss Bites

Makes: 12

Ingredients:
- 1/3 cup canned pumpkin puree
- 1 cup oats
- 1 scoop vanilla protein powder
- 1/8 cup pure maple syrup or raw honey
- 1/2 teaspoon cinnamon
- 1/2 teaspoon pumpkin pie spice

Directions:
1. Combine everything well.

2. Scoop 1 tablespoon of mixture and roll into ball (it will be sticky!) Place on parchment paper lined pan or plate.

3. Refrigerate for at least 1 hour.

4. Mix 1/2 scoop vanilla whey protein with 1 tablespoon unsweetened almond milk. Drizzle on top of each bite.

Everyone must take time to sit and watch the leaves turn.
~ Elizabeth Lawrence ~

Pumpkin Pie Protein Shake!

Serves: 1

BEST protein shake I've ever tasted, MUST share!

Ingredients:
- 1 cup unsweetened almond or coconut milk
- 1 scoop vanilla whey
- 2 tablespoons all-natural pumpkin puree
- 1/4 teaspoon vanilla extract
- sprinkle of pumpkin pie spice
- pinch of granulated stevia or a touch of any sweetener you wish
- 1½ cups ice

Directions:
Combine ingredients in a blender and process until smooth. Serve immediately.

Breakfast Pumpkin & Orange Smoothie

Serves: 2

Ingredients:

1 cup Greek vanilla yogurt
3/4 cup canned pumpkin puree, chilled
1/2 cup ice cubes
1/3 cup fresh squeezed orange juice
Pinch of granulated stevia OR 3 drops liquid stevia OR sweetener of choice
1/2 teaspoon ground cinnamon
1/8 teaspoon ground nutmeg
Dash of ground cloves
1 Frozen banana, sliced
Dash of ground cinnamon (optional)

Directions:

Combine yogurt and next 8 ingredients (through banana) in a blender, and process until smooth. Garnish with dash of ground cinnamon, if desired. Serve immediately.

Pumpkin Pie Smoothie

Serves: 1

Ingredients:

- ½ cup pumpkin puree
- ½ medium-sized banana
- ¾ cup fat-free Greek vanilla yogurt
- 1 tablespoon raw honey
- ½ teaspoon pumpkin pie spice
- ¼ teaspoon vanilla extract
- 1 cup crushed ice

Directions:

Place all ingredients in a blender and puree until smooth.

Pumpkin Spice Smoothie

Serves: 1

Ingredients:

- 1 cup unsweetened almond milk
- ½ cup pumpkin puree
- ½ banana
- 1 tablespoon raisins or ½ teaspoon pure maple syrup
- ½ teaspoon vanilla extract
- ¼ teaspoon ground cinnamon
- ⅛ teaspoon ground ginger
- pinch ground nutmeg
- pinch ground cloves
- pinch of allspice

Directions:

1. Place everything in the blender.
2. Blend until smooth
3. Pour into your favorite glass and place a couple tablespoons of coconut whipped cream on top.
4. Sprinkle with cinnamon!

Pumpkin Booty-Building Protein Shake

Serves: 2

Ingredients:

- 1 serving vanilla protein powder (whey-based is preferred)
- 1 cup of homemade pumpkin puree or canned pumpkin
- 1 cup almond milk or coconut milk
- 1 banana, preferably previously peeled and frozen
- 1 teaspoon vanilla extract
- 2 teaspoons pure maple syrup or raw honey
- Pinch of nutmeg-optional

Directions:

1. Blend all ingredients until smooth. Add several ice cubes and blend again, if desired.

Peanut Butter & Pumpkin Smoothie

Serves: 1

Ingredients:

⅓ cup pumpkin
¼ frozen banana
2 tablespoon Peanut Butter (All Natural)
¼ cup coconut milk
½ cup plain greek yogurt
¾ teaspoon vanilla extract
1 teaspoon maple syrup
½ teaspoon stevia or extra 1 teaspoon maple syrup
¾ teaspoon pumpkin pie spice
4 ice cubes

Directions:

1. Blend all the ingredients in your blender. Process until smooth.

Make Ice Cream Nice!

Pumpkin Ice Cream!

Servings: 8

Non-Dairy Packed with Nutrition. Less than 200 calories per serving - Including the chocolate!

Ingredients:

- 8 FROZEN bananas, chopped
- 2 cups all-natural pumpkin puree
  2 tablespoons raw honey or pure maple syrup
- May require 2 tablespoons unsweetened almond milk to get it blended.

Directions:

1. In your high powered blender combine the ingredients.

2. Fill a 9x13 dish with pumpkin mixture. Spread evenly. Freeze 4 hours.

3. Optional: Melt 1/2 cup dark chocolate/cacao and drizzle evenly over Pumpkin Ice Cream.

4. Use scoop to serve immediately or re-freeze, tightly covered.

Pumpkin Spice Latte

(Makes 2 lattes)

Ingredients:

- ‣ 3 cups freshly brewed HOT coffee
- ‣ 1 tablespoon pumpkin spice
- ‣ 2 cups warmed unsweetened vanilla almond milk OR 2 cups warmed coconut milk
- ‣ 1/2 teaspoon vanilla extract
- ‣ 2 tablespoons pure maple syrup

Directions:

1. Combine all ingredients in blender.
2. Blend until frothy.
3. Serve immediately.

Clean Pumpkin Spice Latte for 1

ngredients:

- 1 cup unsweetened almond milk
- 2 tablespoon pumpkin puree (canned or fresh)
- 2 teaspoons maple syrup
- ½ teaspoon pumpkin pie spice
- ½ teaspoon vanilla extract
- ½ cup strong brewed coffee (or 2 shots of espresso)
- Fresh grated nutmeg (optional)

)irections:

. Combine almond milk, pumpkin, maple syrup, pumpkin pie spice and vanilla in a small saucepan over a medium low heat. Whisk everything together.
. As milk begins to simmer, shut off the heat and transfer the milk mixture to a blender.
. Add ½ cup of strong brewed coffee to blender. Blend for 10 seconds or until light and frothy.
. Pour into a coffee mug. Top with nutmeg and enjoy!

Pumpkin Spice Latte for Agave lovers

Serves: 2

Ingredients:

▸ 2 cups unsweetened almond/coconut milk
▸ 2 tablespoons canned pumpkin puree
▸ 1-2 tablespoons agave nectar
▸ 1 Tablespoon quality vanilla extract
▸ 1/2 teaspoon pumpkin pie spice
▸ 1-4 shots espresso or 2 cups very strong HOT coffee

Directions:

1. Brew your espresso or very strong coffee.

2. While it's brewing, in a small saucepan, combine milk, pumpkin, agave and pie spice, whisking gently over medium heat until well blended and very hot, but NOT boiling.

3. Remove the mixture from the heat. Add 1 tablespoon of high quality vanilla extract.

4. Carefully pour the hot mix into a blender or use an immersion blender and blend until frothy.

5. Pour about a cup of the frothy pumpkin milk mixture into your favorite mug and add coffee to the top. Stir gently. I like to dust with a bit of cinnamon.

Eat your pureed pumpkin, don't feel feel guilty about it!

Canned pumpkin puree – not pumpkin pie filling --

Is low in calories and good source of fiber and vitamin A.

Clean Pumpkin Latte made with Stevia

Serves: 1

Ingredients:

- 1/2 cup unsweetened vanilla almond milk
- 3 tablespoons pumpkin puree
- 1 teaspoon pumpkin pie spice
- 1/2 teaspoon vanilla extract
- 2-3 drops of liquid stevia OR 1 pinch granulated stevia (or sweetener of choice)
- 8 ounces brewed HOT coffee (or 1-2 shots of espresso)
- sprinkle of cinnamon

Directions:

1. In a saucepan, mix together almond milk and pumpkin. Cook on medium heat on the stovetop, for just a minute.
2. Remove from heat, stir in vanilla, spices, and sweetener, place in a cup and use a frother to foam the milk. You can also use a blender, just process for 30 seconds or until frothy.
3. Pour coffee into a large mug, add the foamy milk mixture on top.
4. Sprinkle with cinnamon. Enjoy!

Protein Pumpkin Spice Latte

{Directions for HOT or ICED}

Serves: 1

☆ Hot Latte

In blender combine:

▸ 1/2 cup HOT unsweetened almond milk or HOT coconut milk
▸ 1 tsp vanilla extract
▸ 1/4 teaspoon stevia granules/3 drops liquid or sweetener of choice
▸ 1 cup freshly brewed HOT coffee
▸ 1/2 teaspoon pumpkin pie spice (make your own pumpkin pie spice: 1/4 tsp cinnamon, 1/8 tsp ginger, 1/8 tsp nutmeg, & a sprinkle of allspice)
▸ 1/2 tablespoon all-natural pumpkin puree
▸ 1/2 scoop vanilla protein powder (Protein powder optional)

Directions:

Blend until frothy.

☆ Iced Latte

In blender combine:

▸ 1/2 cup COLD unsweetened almond milk or COLD unsweetened coconut milk
▸ 1 teaspoon vanilla extract
▸ 1/4 teaspoon stevia granules or sweetener of choice
▸ 1 cup coffee
▸ 1/2 teaspoon pumpkin pie spice {make your own pumpkin pie spice: 1/4 tsp cinnamon, 1/8 tsp ginger, 1/8 tsp nutmeg, & a sprinkle of allspice}
▸ 1/2 tablespoon all-natural pumpkin puree
▸ 1/2 scoop vanilla protein powder (protein powder completely optional)
▸ 1 ½ cups ice

Directions:

Blend until slushy, add more ice if needed.

{ Two - Pumpkin Mornings }

"Delicious autumn! My very soul is wedded to it, and if I were a bird I would fly about the earth seeking the successive autumns."

~ George Eliot ~

Pumpkin & Spice Granola

Makes 8 servings

Ingredients:

- 3 cups old-fashioned rolled oats
- 1 cup pecan halves or pieces
- 1 1/2 teaspoons ground cinnamon
- 1/2 teaspoon ground ginger
- 1/8 teaspoon ground nutmeg
- tiny sprinkle of ground cloves
- 1/4 teaspoon sea salt
- 1/3 cup pure pumpkin puree
- 1/2 cup pure maple syrup
- 3 tablespoons melted virgin coconut oil
- 1 teaspoon pure vanilla extract

Directions:

1. Preheat oven to 300°F. Line a large rimmed flat baking sheet with parchment paper.

2. Place oats, pecans, cinnamon, ginger, nutmeg, cloves and salt in a large bowl; stir to mix.

3. Combine pumpkin puree, maple syrup, coconut oil and vanilla; stir until well combined.

4. Add pumpkin mixture to oat mixture; combine well. Spread mixture in prepared baking sheet.

5. Bake 45 minutes, stirring every 15 minutes. Bake about 15 minutes more or until toasted, stirrin every 5 minutes. (Ovens vary. Be careful not to burn.)

6. Let cool completely. (Granola will become crispier when cool.)

7. Store in an airtight container at room temperature.

Pumpkin Protein Waffles

Makes 2 servings

Ingredients:

- 1 cup egg whites
- 3/4 cup pumpkin puree
- 1/2 cup almond flour
- 1 scoop vanilla protein powder
- 2 tablespoons flax seed
- Sweetener of choice-to taste. I used 2 teaspoons granulated stevia
- 1 teaspoon coconut oil
- 1/8 teaspoon ginger
- 1/4 teaspoon nutmeg
- 1/2 teaspoon cinnamon
- 1/2 teaspoon pumpkin pie spice
- 1/4 teaspoon baking soda
- 1/4 teaspoon sea salt

Directions:

1. Pre-heat waffle maker to medium low heat.

2. Stir the pumpkin into the egg whites until combined.

3. Sift dry ingredients separately, then add to the wet ingredients.

4. Pour in 1/2 cup measure of waffle mix evenly onto waffle iron.

5. Close lid and set timer for 2-3 minutes. (Time will vary depending on waffle maker.)

6. I topped mine with Pecans.

For the Love
of Pancakes!

Spiced Pumpkin Protein Pancakes

Serves: 2 (4-5 pancakes each)

Ingredients:
- 1¼ cups Oat Flour
- 2 scoops vanilla whey powder
- 2 teaspoon granulated stevia or 10 drops liquid stevia(or sweetener of choice)
- 1 tablespoon Baking Powder
- 1/2 teaspoon Sea Salt
- 1 tbsp Cinnamon
- 1/4 teaspoon Allspice
- 1/4 teaspoon Nutmeg
- 4 egg Whites
- 1/2 cup pumpkin puree
- 1½ cups unsweetened Almond Milk

Directions:
1. Preheat griddle to medium heat.
2. Mix oat flour, stevia, baking powder, salt, cinnamon, allspice and nutmeg in a bowl.
3. Whisk egg whites and pumpkin. Mix in Almond milk.
4. Combine all ingredients. Mix well.
5. Spray griddle with non-stick spray.
6. Scoop batter with a 1/4 cup measuring cup onto griddle.
7. Cook about 3 minutes per side.

Grain-Free Pumpkin Pancakes

Makes 5-6 pancakes (2 servings)

Ingredients:
- 2 eggs, whisked
- 1/2 cup pumpkin purée
- 2 tablespoon raw honey
- 1/4 teaspoon of pure vanilla extract
- 2/3 cup almond flour
- 1 teaspoon pumpkin pie spice
- 1/4 teaspoon baking soda
- coconut oil to grease your griddle or pan

Directions:
1. In a small bowl, combine the two whisked eggs, pumpkin puree, honey and vanilla.
2. In a medium-size bowl, mix together the almond flour, pumpkin pie spice and baking soda
3. Pour combined wet ingredients into the medium bowl with dry ingredients, and mix into a batter
4. Spoon onto a LOW HEAT griddle or pan, smooth out into an even layer
5. Allow to cook slowly until pancakes are browned on both sides

Pumpkin Facts:
Pumpkin flesh contains L-tryptophan, a chemical compound that triggers feelings of well-being and happiness.

Whole Wheat Pumpkin Pancakes

Serves: 6

Ingredients:

- 1½ cups almond milk
- 1 cup pumpkin puree
- 3 whole eggs
- 1 tablespoon melted coconut oil
- 1 tablespoon raw honey
- 1 teaspoon pure vanilla extract
- 2 cups whole-wheat flour
- 3 teaspoon baking powder
- 2 teaspoon ground cinnamon
- 1 teaspoon baking soda
- 1 teaspoon ground allspice
- pinch of sea salt
- Olive oil or coconut oil cooking spray

Directions:

1. In a large bowl whisk milk, pumpkin, eggs, oil, 1 tbsp honey and vanilla.

2. In a medium bowl whisk flour, baking powder, cinnamon, baking soda, allspice and salt.

3. Add to pumpkin mixture and stir until just combined; set aside. Note: batter will be thin.

4. Spray a large nonstick skillet with cooking spray and heat on medium-high. Working in batches, add batter to skillet in 1/4 cup portions.

5. Cook until bubbles form around edges.

6. Flip and cook until golden brown.

Protein Packed Pumpkin Pancakes

Serves: 2

Ingredients:

- 1 cup rolled oats
- ¾ egg whites (about 6)
- ½ cup Cottage cheese
- ¼ cup pumpkin puree
- 1 tablespoon maple syrup
- 1 teaspoon pumpkin pie spice

Directions:

1. Place everything into the blender and blend until you have a batter.
2. Heat a nonstick skillet over medium heat.
3. Lightly coat the pan with coconut oil or cooking spray and drop ¼ cup rounds of batter onto the pan.
4. Cook until edges are bubbling and then flip and cook several more minutes or until edges are golden brown and pancakes are cooked through.

Pumpkin Protein Pancakes

BEST weekend pancakes!
{Make extra to freeze for the week}

Recipe for each 1 serving: (makes 4 medium pancakes)

Mix dry ingredients with fork:
- 1/2 cup ground oat flour (oatmeal processed in blender or food processor)
- 1 scoop vanilla protein powder
- 1/2 teaspoon baking powder
- a good pinch of cinnamon
- tiny pinch of nutmeg

{Combine dry ingredients well}

Wet ingredients:
- 3-4 egg whites or 2 whole eggs
- 2 Tbsp unsweetened almond milk
- 1/4 tsp pure vanilla extract
- 1/4 cup Pumpkin puree

Directions:
1. Whisk wet ingredients very well with a fork.
2. Combine wet and dry ingredients to make a batter.
3. Lightly coat the pan with coconut oil or cooking spray and drop ¼ cup rounds of batter onto the pan.
4. Cook until edges are bubbling and then flip and cook several more minutes or until edges are golden brown and pancakes are cooked through.
5. While your pancakes are cooking, you can drop 3 dark cacao chips on each one.
6. I served mine with a dollop of whipped coconut cream, whipped with stevia and cinnamon.

Coconut Whipped Cream

Directions:

- Place a 5.4 oz can of coconut cream, or a 15-16 oz can of full fat coconut milk in the REFRIGERATOR overnight.

- The cream whips best if your mixing bowl & beaters are very cold as well. I place mine in the FREEZER for at least 20 minutes prior to prep.

(Actually, I store my beaters in the freezer...because...whipped cream all the time!!)

- Open can carefully without shaking or flipping upside down.

Spoon out the top layer of opaque white coconut cream that has gathered to the top of the can. The bright white stuff is what you will use. (The leftover watery liquid can be used in a smoothie.)

Flavor Ideas: 1 teaspoon pure vanilla extract, a bit of pure vanilla bean, pure almond extract, OR cinnamon… any tiny amount of flavor you want to use here. I have even made chocolate cream by adding a tablespoon or two of unsweetened cacao powder. Choose your favorite & try something new each time!

I use 10 drops liquid stevia or about a 1/2 teaspoon stevia granules for my sweetener. Sweetness is a personal preference. Served with fresh, ripe berries I do not believe the cream needs a lot of sweetener. The amount / sweetener type is up to you.

Beat all ingredients with an electric hand mixer, for several minutes on high, moving the beaters up & down often to infuse air into the cream. An airy cream will form...time to serve!

Whole Wheat Pumpkin Bread

Makes 1 loaf (16 servings)

Ingredients:

- 1½ cups whole wheat flour
- 1 teaspoon baking powder
- 1/2 teaspoon baking soda
- 1/2 teaspoon table salt
- 1/2 teaspoon ground ginger
- 1/4 teaspoon ground cloves
- 2 teaspoons ground cinnamon
- 1 egg, beaten
- 3/4 cup organic sucanat (dried sugar cane juice)
- 3/4 cup plain greek yogurt
- 3/4 cup canned pure pumpkin puree
- 3 tablespoon coconut oil
- 1½ teaspoons pure vanilla extract
- 1/2 cup chopped walnuts or pecans

Directions:

1. Preheat oven to 350°F. Spray bottom of 8×4-inch loaf pan with cooking spray.
2. In large bowl, mix flour, baking powder, cinnamon, baking soda, salt, ginger and cloves.
3. In medium bowl mix egg, sucanat, yogurt, pumpkin, oil and vanilla until well blended.
4. Add to flour mixture, stirring until just combined. Stir in nuts.
5. Pour batter into pan.
6. Bake 50 to 60 minutes or until toothpick inserted in center comes out clean.
7. Cool in pan 15-20 minutes.

AMAZING Grain-Free Chocolate Chip Pumpkin Bread

This HEALTHY version might be the best you've EVER had!

Makes 10-12 servings

Ingredients:

- ½ cup coconut flour
- ½ teaspoon sea salt
- ½ teaspoon baking soda
- 2 teaspoons pumpkin pie spice
- ½ cup all-natural pumpkin puree
- 5 Medjool dates
- 2 Tbsp pure maple syrup
- 6 whole eggs
- 1 tablespoon vanilla extract
- ¼ cup coconut oil, melted
- ½ cup mini dark chocolate chips

Directions:

1. Preheat the oven to 350°F and line a loaf pan with parchment paper, or grease with coconut oil.
2. Pit the dates and place in small sauce pan with 1 tablespoon of water, bring to a low simmer, for about 6-8 minutes until soft, then mash with a fork.
3. Add the maple syrup to the date mixture to make a paste.
4. In a large bowl, whisk the coconut flour, baking soda, sea salt and pumpkin pie spice.
5. In a small bowl, mix the pumpkin, eggs and vanilla. Add the date paste and whisk until well combined.
6. Add the wet ingredients to the dry.
7. Add the melted coconut oil and fold in the chocolate chips.
8. Pour the batter into the bread pan and bake for 45 to 55 minutes.
9. Cool on a wire rack and enjoy a warm slice!

Pumpkin Protein Oat Muffins

Breakfast... Snacks... Lunch... More Snacks...

Makes: 12 muffins

Ingredients:

- 2 cups dry rolled oats
- 2 scoops protein powder {I used vanilla whey }
- 2 cups all-natural pumpkin puree { one 15 oz can }
- ¼ cup unsweetened applesauce
- 1 cup unsweetened almond milk
- 2 whole eggs, or 6 egg whites
- 1 teaspoon stevia granules or sweetener of choice
- 1 teaspoon baking powder
- 1/2 teaspoon vanilla extract
- 1/2 teaspoon cinnamon
- 1/2 cup cacao chips, or Lily's brand sweetened with stevia

Directions:

1. Preheat oven to 350°F
2. In large bowl combine all ingredients well. Scoop batter evenly into sprayed muffin tins {I used non-stick (important that they are non stick!) cupcake liners}
3. Bake 17-18 minutes, until muffin centers are just set.
4. Enjoy!

Pumpkin Facts: The Beta carotene present in pumpkin seeds and flesh has antioxidant and anti-inflammatory properties. Regular consumption of pumpkin can protect against joint inflammation and arthritis.

Seriously.
Make.
These.

Flourless Double Chocolate PB Muffins

Flourless-Moist-Gooey-SIMPLE

Makes 12 regular muffins

Ingredients:

- 2 large beaten eggs (room temp)
- 2 cups PB or Almond Butter (creamy smooth-room temp works best)
- 1/2 cup pure maple syrup
- 1½ cups pure pumpkin puree
- 6 tablespoons unsweetened cacao powder
- 2 teaspoons baking soda
- 2 teaspoons vanilla extract
- 1/2 to 3/4 cups cacao, or dark chocolate chips. (I love Lily's brand sweetened with stevia available: CleanFoodCrush.com/lilys)

Directions:

1. Preheat oven to 350°F
2. Spray muffin tray or line with parchment liners.
3. Combine all ingredients, just until smooth; adding chocolate chips last.
4. Fill muffin tins 3/4 full. I use a large ice cream scoop, so they are each even portions.
5. Bake in preheated oven for 25-35 minutes until toothpick comes out clean.
6. They are VERY moist if they are NOT over-baked.

Not too sweet.

Rich & delicious!

Grain-Free Pumpkin Muffins

Must Try! PROMISE these are SO good!
My children LOVE these on cool Fall mornings
12 Muffins

Ingredients:

‣ 3/4 cup pumpkin puree
‣ 1 cup all-natural almond butter
‣ 1/3 cup raw honey or pure maple syrup)
‣ 2 whole eggs
‣ 1 tablespoon pumpkin pie spice (You can always make your own pumpkin pie spice by using 2 tsp ground cinnamon, 1/2 tsp ground ginger, and 1/4 tsp ground nutmeg)
‣ 1 tsp baking soda
‣ 1/3 cup taco chips or dark chocolate chips. I used Lily's brand sweetened with stevia. (Optional)

Directions:

1. Preheat over to 350°F. Grease or spray your mini muffin pan with coconut oil.
2. Combine all ingredients until batter is smooth. If using chocolate chips fold them in last.
3. Bake for about 16-18 minutes. Keep an eye on them!

Pumpkin Facts: Like their orange comrades the sweet potato, the carrot and the butternut squash (to name a few), pumpkins boast the antioxidant beta-carotene, which may play a role in cancer prevention, according to the National Cancer Institute.

{ Three - Pumpkin Sides }

*"I cannot endure to waste anything as precious as autumn
sunshine by staying in the house.
So I spend almost all the daylight hours in the open air."*

~ Nathaniel Hawthorne ~

Make your own Pumpkin Puree!

Ingredients:

‣ 2 Small Sugar Pumpkins

Directions:

1. Cut the pumpkins in half. With a spoon, scrape out the seeds and pulp from the center.
2. Place all the seeds into a bowl (you can roast them later).
3. Place pumpkin pieces on a baking sheet (face down) and roast in a 350°F oven for 45 minutes, or until pumpkin is tender. It should be light golden brown when ready.
4. Peel off the skin from the pumpkin pieces. In a food processor, process a few chunks at a time. A blender will work too if you add a bit of water.
5. Pulse the pumpkin until smooth. If it's dry, add in a few tablespoons of water.
6. Dump the puree into a bowl and continue pureeing until all the pumpkin is done.
7. You can use the puree immediately or store it in the freezer for later use.
8. To store in the freezer, place 1 cupful of pumpkin into each plastic storage bag.

Pumpkin Mashed Potatoes

Serves: 6

Ingredients:

- 6 red potatoes, chopped
- 1/2 tablespoon olive oil
- 2 cloves garlic, minced
- 1½ cups pumpkin puree
- 1/2 cup unsweetened Almond milk
- 2 tbsp coconut oil or grass-fed butter
- 2 teaspoons sea salt
  Freshly ground black pepper, to taste
  chives for garnish

Directions:

1. Bring a large pot of water to a boil over high heat and boil potatoes for 18 to 22 minutes or until fork tender.

2. Drain and place in a large bowl.

3. Meanwhile, heat olive oil over low heat in a skillet and sauté garlic for 1 minute.

4. Drain and mash potato in a large bowl with a fork.

5. Mix in pumpkin puree, almond milk, Grass-fed/butter, black pepper, and salt.

6. Mix all ingredients into the large bowl. Mash until desired consistency. Serve.

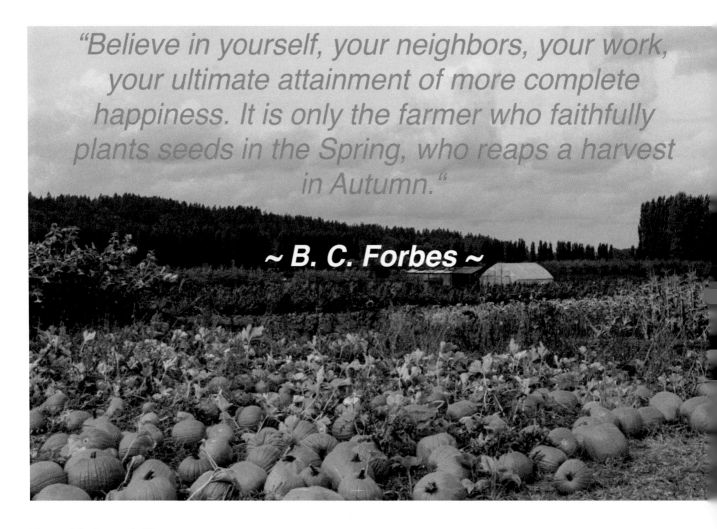

"Believe in yourself, your neighbors, your work, your ultimate attainment of more complete happiness. It is only the farmer who faithfully plants seeds in the Spring, who reaps a harvest in Autumn."

~ B. C. Forbes ~

Creamy Coconut Pumpkin Mashed Potatoes

Serves: 6

Ingredients:

‣ 2½ pounds potatoes, peeled
‣ 2 tablespoons coconut oil or grass-fed butter
‣ 1/4 cup coconut cream
‣ 15 ounce can pumpkin puree
‣ 1/2 teaspoon ground cinnamon
‣ 1/2 teaspoon ground ginger
‣ 1/8 teaspoon ground nutmeg
‣ 1/8 teaspoon ground cloves
‣ 2 tablespoons maple syrup
‣ 1/2 teaspoon sea salt
‣ freshly ground black pepper
‣ minced fresh chives or parsley as garnish

Directions:

1. Place the potatoes in a large pot and cover completely with water.

2. Bring to boil, turn the heat to medium-low and cook potatoes for about 20 minutes or until you can easily pierce with a fork.

3. Drain water.

4. Mash the potatoes. Mash and stir in the remaining ingredients to the mashed potatoes until smooth.

5. Taste and adjust seasonings if needed.

Pumpkin FRIES!

Serves: 6

Ingredients:

‣ 2 small pie pumpkins

Salty Pumpkin Fries:

‣ 2 teaspoons garlic powder
‣ 1/4 teaspoon cayenne pepper
‣ 1 teaspoon onion powder
‣ 1 tablespoon olive oil
‣ sea salt to taste

Sweet Fries:

‣ 2 teaspoons pumpkin pie spice
‣ 2 tablespoons pure maple syrup

Spicy Fries:

‣ 1 tablespoon pure maple syrup
‣ 1 tablespoon Sriracha (less if you don't
   want as much spice)

Directions:

1. Preheat oven to 400°F.

2. Peel & remove seeds then cut into ½ inch fries.

3. Coat your pumpkin in desired spices. (salty, spicy, or sweet.

4. Arrange the fries in a single layer on a parchment lined cookie sheet.

5. Roast for approximately 35 minutes, flipping fries halfway through.

SALTY PUMPKIN FRIES

▸ Place your cut pumpkin and olive oil in a mixing bowl.
▸ Toss by hand until the pumpkin is well coated in all the oil and spices.

SWEET PUMPKIN FRIES

▸ Place your cut pumpkin into a mixing bowl.
▸ Add maple syrup and toss by hand until your pumpkin is well coated.

SPICY PUMPKIN FRIES

▸ Toss pumpkin fries, maple syrup and Sriracha in a large bowl.
▸ These are SPICY!!!

{ Arrange in single layer on baking sheet, roast at 400°F for 35 minutes, flipping fries halfway through. }

Pumpkin for POST-WORKOUT!

Ever heard of bananas being touted as nature's energy bar? Turns out, a cup of cooked pumpkin has more of the refueling nutrient potassium, with 564 milligrams to a banana's 422.

Spicy Roasted Pumpkin

Serves: 4

Ingredients:

‣ 2 lbs. fresh pumpkin, peeled & seeded
‣ 2 tablespoons olive oil
‣ 1/2 teaspoon sea salt
‣ 1 teaspoon fresh ground black pepper
‣ 1 teaspoon ground cumin

Directions:

1. Pre-heat oven to 400°F.
2. Quarter and then carefully peel and seed the pumpkin.
3. Cut into 2 inch cubes.
4. Place pumpkin onto flat roasting tray
5. Add the olive oil, salt, pepper & cumin - combine well, making sure that all the pumpkin pieces are coated in olive oil.
6. Bake in the oven for about 30 to 45 minutes or until the pumpkin is soft & also tinged brown at the edges. Stirring/tossing once during roasting time.

Roasted Pumpkin Slices

Ingredients:

- 1 small pumpkin or 1/4 large pumpkin
- 1 tablespoon olive oil
- sea salt
  ground clove
  ground cinnamon
  ground nutmeg
- 1 tablespoon raw honey

Directions:

1. Heat oven to 400°F.
2. Using a large metal spoon, scoop out the seeds and insides of the pumpkin. Save the seeds for roasting.
3. Use a sharp knife to cut slices of pumpkin, about 1-inch thick (I love to make these a crescent moon shape for the kids!)
4. Place pumpkin slices on flat baking sheet. Drizzle with olive oil and rub on both sides of pumpkin. Season with salt, spices and honey. Roast for 20-25 minutes, depending on thickness of pumpkin slices.

Raw pumpkin has a rich flavor that makes it a good snack. The best way to eat it is to slice the pumpkin into cubes, but you can also eat raw canned pumpkin.

However, so you don't tire of it, you can add other ingredients without changing its nutritional value. Sprinkle cinnamon to give it a dessert-like flavor without all of the fat and sugar.

{ Four - Pumpkin Soups & Chili }

"Autumn is a second spring when every leaf is a flower."

~ Albert Camus ~

Simple Pumpkin Soup with a Kick!

Serves: 6

Ingredients:

▸ 3 cups organic chicken broth

▸ 1 (15 ounce) can pumpkin puree

▸ 1 yellow onion, diced

▸ 2 cloves garlic, minced

▸ 1-2 teaspoons Cajun seasoning (depending on the kick you desire! :)

▸ 1 cup unsweetened almond milk or coconut milk

Directions:

1. Heat chicken broth, pumpkin puree, onion, garlic, and Cajun seasoning to a boil in a saucepan over medium-high heat.

2. Reduce heat to low and simmer for 45 to 60 minutes, stirring every 15 minutes.

3. Stir in unsweetened almond milk or coconut milk a few minutes before serving.

4. Sea salt & fresh ground Pepper to taste.

World's Best Pumpkin Soup

Serves: 6

Ingredients:

3 tablespoons extra-virgin olive oil

1 onion, roughly chopped

2 cloves garlic, chopped

2 teaspoons cumin

1/4 teaspoons cayenne pepper

1/2 of a small pumpkin, peeled & chopped into large cubes

1 sweet potato peeled & cubed

3 stalks celery, chopped

4 cups organic chicken stock

Directions:

. Heat oil in the bottom of a big stock pot. Add onion and cook over low heat until the onion is translucent, about 5 minutes. Add garlic & cumin and stir for another minute or so.

. Add pumpkin, sweet potato, celery, and stock and bring to a low simmer. Cover partially and let it cook on the stovetop for about 20-25 minutes, or until the veggies are soft.

. Let it cool slightly, then pour it into the blender in batches or use an immersion blender to puree the soup. Return to the pot and season to taste.

Pumpkin Facts:
A 1-cup serving of Pumpkin contains 7 grams of fiber.

Curry Pumpkin Soup

Serves: 6

Ingredients:

- ▸ 2 tablespoons unrefined coconut oil
- ▸ 3 tablespoons coconut flour
- ▸ 2 tablespoons curry powder
- ▸ 4 cups vegetable broth
- ▸ 1 (29 ounce) can pumpkin
- ▸ 1½ cups full-fat natural Greek yogurt
- ▸ 2 tablespoons soy sauce (liquid aminos made by: Braggs as a GREAT substitute)
- ▸ 2 tablespoons raw honey
- ▸ salt and pepper to taste
- ▸ 2 tablespoons pumpkin seeds (optional)

Directions:

1. Melt oil in a large pot over medium heat.
2. Stir in flour and curry powder until smooth.
3. Cook, stirring until mixture begins to bubble.
4. Gradually whisk in broth and cook until thickened.
5. Stir in pumpkin and yogurt.
6. Season with soy sauce (liquid aminos), honey, sea salt, and pepper.
7. Bring just to a boil and remove from heat.
8. Garnish with roasted pumpkin seeds.

The GREAT Pumpkin Soup

Serves: 6

Ingredients:

- 2 whole pie pumpkins
- 1 quart vegetable Or organic chicken stock
- 1/2 cup full-fat plain Greek yogurt
- ¼ tsp nutmeg
- 1/3 cup REAL maple syrup
- Sea salt To Taste

Directions:

1. Preheat oven to 300°F.
2. Place pumpkins on a flat baking sheet and roast until slightly soft.
3. Allow to cool, then slice in half and scoop out seeds and pulp. Scoop pumpkin flesh into a bowl.
4. In a large stockpot, heat the pumpkin flesh with the stock and maple syrup until simmering.
5. Mash the pumpkin, then transfer the mixture to your blender or food processor (or use an immersion/stick blender) and puree until smooth.
6. Add yogurt and nutmeg... blend again.
7. Reheat & serve!

Southwestern Pumpkin Black Bean Soup

Serves: 6

Ingredients:

- 2 tablespoon extra-virgin olive oil

- 1 medium onion, diced small

- 3 cups canned or packaged vegetable stock

- 1 can (15 ounces) black beans, drained & rinsed

- 1 can (14 1/2 ounces) diced tomatoes in juice

- 2 cans (15 ounces each) all-natural pumpkin puree

- 1 cup Plain Greek Yogurt

- 1/2 teaspoon cayenne pepper

- 1 tablespoon curry powder

- 1½ teaspoons ground cumin

- Sea salt

- Fresh lime as garnish

- Green onion or Fresh Cilantro as a garnish

Directions:

1. Heat a large stockpot over medium heat.

2. Add oil. Once oil is hot, add onion. Sauté onions 4-5 minutes.

3. Add broth, tomatoes, black beans and pumpkin puree. Stir to combine ingredients and bring soup to a boil.

4. Reduce heat to medium low and stir in yogurt, curry, cumin, cayenne and salt, to taste.

5. Simmer 5 minutes, Serve with your FAV southwestern garnish!

Coconut Pumpkin Soup

Serves: 6

Ingredients:

- 2 medium pumpkins

- 2 cups organic chicken broth

- 1 cup water

- 1/4 cup REAL maple syrup

- 1 teaspoon cinnamon

- 1/2 teaspoon nutmeg

- 1/2 teaspoon sea salt

- 1/2 teaspoon freshly ground ginger

- 1 cup Full-Fat Coconut Milk

Directions:

1. Preheat oven to 350°F.

2. Cut the 2 medium pumpkins in half, scoop out the seeds, and place skin-side down on a flat baking sheet.

3. Bake for 35 to 45 minutes, or until soft. Scoop out the pumpkin flesh into food processor and puree until smooth.

4. Pour pureed pumpkin into a saucepan and add the chicken broth, water, maple syrup and spices.

5. Bring to a boil, then reduce to a simmer and simmer for 30 minutes.

6. Remove the soup from heat and stir in the coconut milk.

7. Serve.

Sweet Potato & Pumpkin Soup

Serves: 6

Ingredients:

- 2 teaspoons cumin powder
- 2 teaspoons dried oregano
- 1 tablespoon ground fennel
- 1/2 teaspoon crushed red pepper
- 1/2 teaspoon sea salt
- 1/2 teaspoon freshly ground black pepper
- 1 clove garlic, minced
- 2 tablespoons extra-virgin olive oil, divided
- 1 medium pumpkin
- 4 sweet potatoes
- 1 large onion, diced
- 1½ quarts chicken broth

Autumn is a perfect time for reflection, and also for joy.

Directions:

1. Preheat oven to 400°F.

2. Combine: cumin, oregano, fennel, red pepper, salt, pepper, garlic, and 1 tablespoon olive oil to form a paste.

3. Wash pumpkin and cut into 2-inch wide wedges, scraping away seeds. Peel potatoes and cut each potato lengthwise into 6 wedges. Smear the pumpkin and the potatoes with the spice paste and place in a baking dish.

4. Roast in preheated oven 30 to 40 minutes, until tender and just beginning to blacken at the thinnest points.

5. Meanwhile, in a large pot over medium heat, saute' the onion in the remaining 1 tablespoon olive oil until translucent.

6. Chop pumpkin and potatoes into smaller chunks and puree in a blender or food processor with some of the chicken broth until smooth. Be sure to scrape the roasted spice paste off the baking dish and include it in the puree. It may be necessary to deglaze the dish with a little chicken broth.

7. Pour the pureed vegetables into the pot with the onions, and stir in additional chicken stock as needed to achieve the desired consistency. Heat through.

Harvest Pumpkin Soup

Serves: 6

Ingredients:

- 1 tablespoon unrefined coconut oil
- 1 (3 pound) pumpkin - peeled
- seeded, and cut into small pieces
- 2 tablespoons raw honey
- 1 tablespoon yellow curry powder
- 20 ounces chicken broth
- Plain greek yogurt
- Toasted pumpkin seeds

Directions:

1. Melt the coconut oil in a large pot over medium heat.

2. Add the pumpkin, honey, and curry powder to the oil; cook and stir until the pumpkin caramelizes, 6 to 10 minutes.

3. Pour the chicken broth over the mixture; bring to a boil, and cook until the pumpkin is tender, about 20 minutes more.

4. Pour the soup into a blender, filling the pitcher no more than halfway. Hold the lid of the blender in place; start the blender, using a few quick pulses to get the soup moving before leaving it on to puree. Process in batches until smooth.

5. Garnish each portion of soup with a dollop of yogurt, and a few pumpkin seeds.

Thai Pumpkin Soup

Serves: 4

Ingredients:

- 1 tablespoon extra virgin olive oil
- 1 tablespoon coconut oil
- 1 clove garlic, minced
- 4 shallots, diced
- 2 small fresh red chili peppers, chopped
- 1 tablespoon chopped lemon grass
- 2 1/8 cups organic chicken stock
- 4 cups peeled and diced pumpkin
- 1½ cups unsweetened coconut milk
- 1 bunch fresh basil leaves

Directions:

. In a medium saucepan, heat olive oil and coconut oil over low heat. Cook garlic, shallots, chilies, and lemongrass in oil until fragrant (don't burn the garlic!).

. Stir in chicken stock, coconut milk, and pumpkin; bring to a boil. Cook until pumpkin softens.

. In a blender, blend the soup in batches to a smooth or slightly chunky consistency, depending on your preference. Serve with fresh basil leaves & diced chilies. (optional)

Pumpkin Soup

Delicious White Bean Pumpkin Chili

Serves: 6

Ingredients:

2 tablespoons olive oil

1 yellow onion, diced

1 green bell pepper, diced

1 jalapeno, minced

3 cloves garlic, minced

1½ lb. ground turkey

1 (15 oz) can diced tomatoes

1 (15 oz) can pumpkin puree

2 cups vegetable broth

1 tablespoon chili powder

1 teaspoon ground cumin

1/2 teaspoon sea salt

1 (15 oz) can Great Northern beans

Directions:

In a large stock pot, heat the olive oil on medium high. Add in the onion, bell pepper, jalapeños and garlic. Cook for 5 minutes, stirring constantly.

Next, add the turkey and cook until no longer pink.

Add all remaining ingredients, except beans. Stir to combine.

Bring to a boil, then reduce heat to a simmer, add the beans, cover stock pot and cook on low for 30 minutes - stirring occasionally.

Pumpkin & Grass Fed Beef Chili

Serves 6-8

Ingredients:

- 2 pounds grass-fed ground beef
- 1 large onion, diced
- 1 green bell pepper, diced
- 2 (15 ounce) cans kidney beans, drained
- 1 (46 fluid ounce) can tomato juice
- 1 (28 ounce) can peeled and diced tomatoes with juice
- 1/2 cup pumpkin puree
- 1 tablespoon pumpkin pie spice
- 1 tablespoon chili powder
- 1/4 cup raw honey

Directions:

1. In a large stockpot over medium heat, cook beef until brown; drain well.
2. Stir in onion and bell pepper and cook 4-5 minutes.
3. Stir in beans, tomato juice, diced tomatoes and pumpkin puree.
4. Season with pumpkin pie spice, chili powder and sugar.
5. Simmer, covered on low 1 hour.

Lean Turkey Chili

Serves: 6

Ingredients:

- 1 tablespoon olive oil
- 1 cup diced onion
- 1/2 cup diced green bell pepper
- 1/2 cup diced yellow bell pepper
- 2 cloves garlic, minced
- 1 pound lean ground turkey
- 1 (14.5 ounce) can diced tomatoes
- 2 cups pumpkin puree
- 1½ tablespoons chili powder
- 1/2 teaspoon ground black pepper
- ¼ teaspoon sea salt

Directions:

1. Heat the oil in a large skillet over medium heat. Sauté the onion, green bell pepper, yellow bell pepper, and garlic until tender.
2. Stir in turkey and cook until evenly brown.
3. Drain and mix in tomatoes and pumpkin.
4. Season with chili powder, pepper, and salt.
5. Reduce heat to low, cover, and simmer 20 minutes.
6. Serve topped with diced avocado, and cilantro.

Turkey and Roasted Pumpkin Chili

Serves: 4

Ingredients:

- 1 Medium Pumpkin, peeled, seeded, and cut into 1/2 inch cubes
- 2 tablespoon extra virgin olive oil-divided use
- Sea salt to taste
- 1 lb. ground turkey
- 2 medium carrots, peeled and chopped
- 2 medium celery stalks, chopped
- 1 large yellow onion, diced
- 1 tablespoon. chili powder
- 1 teaspoon ground cumin
- 1 tsp unsweetened cacao powder
- ¼ teaspoon ground cinnamon
- 4 cups organic chicken broth
- diced avocado and cilantro for garnish

Directions:

. Preheat oven to 400°F.

. Toss Pumpkin with 1 tablespoon olive oil and a big pinch of sea salt.

. On a flat-rimmed baking sheet roast for 20-25 minutes until tender and lightly browned. Stir/turn once during roasting time.

. Heat remaining olive oil in a large stockpot over medium heat. Add ground turkey and cook, crumbling with a wooden spoon, until cooked through about 5 mins.

. Add carrots, celery, onion, and garlic (can add any other veggies you might have on hand as well). Cook covered for 6-8 mins until veggies are bright in color and slightly tender, stirring occasionally.

. Add chili powder, cumin, cacao powder and cinnamon. Cook for an additional minute.

. Add broth and bring to a boil. Reduce heat and simmer for 5-10mins to blend flavors.

Stir in roasted pumpkin. Season to taste with sea salt.

Garnish with avocado and cilantro if desired.

Crock-Pot Pumpkin & Beans

Serves: 8
Soooo SIMPLE & delish! Even better the next day

Ingredients:

‣ 2 tablespoons olive oil
‣ 1 medium onion, diced
‣ 1 yellow or orange bell pepper, diced
‣ 3 garlic cloves, minced
‣ 2 cans (15 ounces each) black beans, rinsed and drained
‣ 1 can (15 ounces) pumpkin puree
‣ 1 can (14-1/2 ounces) diced tomatoes, undrained
‣ 3 cups organic chicken broth
‣ 2-1/2 cups cubed cooked turkey breast meat
‣ 2 teaspoons dried parsley flakes
‣ 2 teaspoons chili powder
‣ 1½ teaspoons ground cumin
‣ 1½ teaspoons dried oregano
‣ 1/2 teaspoon sea salt
‣ diced avocado and thinly sliced green onions, optional

Directions:

1. In a large skillet heat oil over medium-high heat. Add onion and pepper; cook until tender.
2. Add garlic; cook 1 minute longer.
3. Transfer to a 5-qt. slow cooker; combine remaining ingredients.
4. Cook, covered, on low 4-5 hours. If desired, top with avocado and green onions.

Pumpkins aren't just for Halloween or for making a Thanksgiving Pie. This vegetable is full of nutrients you can enjoy any time of year.
In fact, it is among the top "fall produce picks" from the Academy of Nutrition and Dietetics.

Clean Food
CRUSH

{ Five - Pumpkin Main Dishes }

*"No spring nor summer beauty hath such grace
As I have seen in one autumnal face."*

~ John Donne ~

Pumpkin Grilled Chicken Breasts:

Serves: 4

Ingredients:

‣ 4 boneless, skinless chicken breasts
‣ 1 cup pumpkin puree
‣ 1 cup organic chicken stock
‣ 1 teaspoon raw honey
‣ 1 teaspoon pure maple syrup
‣ ½ teaspoon cinnamon
‣ ½ teaspoon red pepper flakes
‣ ½ teaspoon curry powder
‣ ½ teaspoon sea salt
‣ ½ teaspoon black pepper

Directions:

1. Place chicken breasts in a shallow baking dish and season with salt and black pepper.
2. In a small bowl mix together pumpkin, chicken stock, honey, maple syrup, cinnamon, red pepper flakes and curry powder.
3. Pour contents over the chicken breasts.
4. Put saran wrap over baking dish and place in fridge to marinate for at least 8 hours or overnight.
5. Heat grill over medium heat.
6. Place chicken breasts on grill and grill with lid closed for 4-5 minutes per side.
7. Cook chicken another 4-5 minutes or until no longer pink inside.

Pumpkin Stuffed Chicken fit for Company

Serves: 6

ngredients:

1 tablespoon olive oil

1 onion, diced

4 cloves garlic, minced

1 cup pumpkin purée

½ cup chopped pecans

½ teaspoon salt

⅛ teaspoon pepper

¼ cup grated ALL-NATURAL Parmesan cheese

1 teaspoon dried thyme leaves

6 boneless, skinless chicken breasts

1 teaspoon paprika

2 tablespoons coconut oil

Directions:

. Preheat oven to 350°F.

. In large saucepan heat olive oil over medium heat. Add onion and garlic; cook and stir until the onion begins to become translucent, about 5 minutes.

. Add pumpkin, pecans, salt, pepper, parmesan, and thyme and remove from heat. Let cool for about 20 minutes so that it's easy to work with.

. Pound chicken breasts until they are about ⅓-inch thick. (I place them in between plastic wrap.) Divide the pumpkin mixture among the chicken breasts and roll up to enclose filling; secure with toothpicks.

In large skillet, heat coconut oil over medium heat. Add chicken; brown on both sides. Place chicken in large baking dish.

Bake, covered with foil, for 30–40 minutes or until chicken is thoroughly cooked. Remove toothpicks and serve immediately.

Pumpkin Turkey Meatloaf

Serves: 6

Ingredients:

- ‣ 1 lb. lean ground turkey
- ‣ 1/2 cup rolled oats
- ‣ 1/2 cup pumpkin purée
- ‣ 3 egg whites
- ‣ 2 teaspoons chili powder
- ‣ 1 teaspoon cinnamon
- ‣ 1 teaspoon pumpkin pie spice

Directions:

1. Preheat the oven to 350°F.
2. Combine all of the ingredients together in a large bowl, and then place inside a loaf pan that's been sprayed with nonstick olive oil spray.
3. Bake at 350°F for about 35 minutes.

Pumpkin seeds are believed to serve as a natural protector against osteoporosis.

Thai Pumpkin Chicken Curry

Serves: 4

Ingredients:

- 1 lb. chicken breast, cubed
- 1 can coconut milk, full fat
- 1 can organic pumpkin puree (15 oz)
- 2 tablespoons coconut oil
- 1 large white onion, chopped
- 2-3 Thai bird's eye chilies, slit but keep in tact
- 3 garlic cloves, minced
- 1 inch ginger, minced
- 1½ teaspoons ground cumin
- 1½ teaspoons ground coriander
- ½ tsp turmeric
- freshly ground salt and pepper to taste
- 2 tbs red curry paste
- 2 tbs fish sauce
- 1 giant handful of Thai basil, chopped
- 1 green bell pepper
- ½ small lime, juice

Directions:

1. Heat coconut oil in a pan on medium heat then add onion, thai chilies and a pinch of salt.
2. Once onion begins to turn golden, add ginger and garlic.
3. After a couple minutes, add the cumin, coriander, turmeric, salt, pepper and curry paste.
4. Add cubed chicken to the pan and stir to coat the meat with the spices.
5. Throw in the bell pepper and Thai basil, give it a quick stir and then pour the coconut milk and canned pumpkin. Add fish sauce.
6. Reduce heat and simmer.
7. Cover and cook for 15 minutes or until chicken is done.

Pumpkin Chicken Enchiladas

Serves: 4
(modified from a Martha Stewart recipe)

Ingredients:

- ▸ 8 gluten-free corn tortillas
- ▸ a few tablespoons of cilantro
- ▸ 1 pound leftover chicken, shredded
- ▸ optional: roasted green chiles, chopped small
- ▸ 6 oz. of white sharp cheddar cheese, shredded

Sauce:

- ▸ 1 can of pumpkin puree (15 oz.)
- ▸ 3-4 cloves of garlic, peeled
- ▸ 1 jalapeño (remove seeds and membranes if you don't need extra heat)
- ▸ 1 teaspoon chile powder
- ▸ 1/2 teaspoon cumin
- ▸ 2 teaspoons of sea salt
- ▸ 1/4 teaspoon of pepper
- ▸ 1½ cups of chicken stock

Directions:

1. Preheat your oven to 425°F.
2. In a blender, puree pumpkin, jalapeño, chicken stock, garlic, chile powder, cumin, salt, and pepper.
3. Place 1 cup of mixture sauce in the bottom of an 8 inch glass casserole dish.
4. In a bowl, combine shredded chicken with green chiles, cilantro, and season with salt and pepper.
5. Place some of the chicken mixture on each tortilla and then lay the tortilla seam side down in the casserole dish.
6. Pour the remaining sauce over the enchiladas. Top with cheese.
7. This recipe is fine without cheese. Martha recommends placing your casserole dish on a baking sheet in the oven to prevent any spills.
8. Bake for 20-25 minutes until cheese is melted and casserole is bubbly.

Creamy Pumpkin Chicken Casserole

Serves: 6

Ingredients:

- 3 cups cooked chicken breast
- 1 large spaghetti squash, cooked
- 1 bell pepper, diced
- 1 onion, diced
- 4 garlic cloves, minced
- 1 teaspoon cinnamon (Ground)
- ½ tsp cumin powder
- ½ tsp coriander powder
- ½ tsp turmeric powder
- sea salt and pepper, adjust to taste
- 1 can organic pumpkin puree
- 1 tbs tomato paste
- 1 can organic coconut milk
- 2 eggs, beaten

Directions:

. To prepare spaghetti squash:
. Preheat oven to 375°F.
. Cut the squash in half, scoop out the seeds, and add a little olive oil, sea salt and pepper to cut sides.
. Place squash cut side down in a baking dish.
. Bake for 45 minutes or until you can easily pierce the skin.

For the casserole:

. In a food processor, add onion, garlic, and blend well.
. Heat oil in a saucepan on medium heat and then add the onion mixture and a pinch of salt. Cook for 5 minutes.
. Add spices, tomato paste and pumpkin puree and mix well.
. Add coconut milk. Stir and simmer for 10 minutes or until the pumpkin puree absorbs the milk.
. Add cooked spaghetti squash strands and chicken to casserole dish. Pour creamy pumpkin mixture on top.
. Add egg, mix well and bake at 350°F for 30-40 minutes.
. Serve.

Grilled Pumpkin

Ingredients:

‣ 1 – 1½ pounds sugar pumpkin
‣ 2 tablespoons olive oil
‣ 1 clove garlic, pressed or minced
‣ kosher salt

Directions:

1. Prepare coals or preheat your gas grill. Cut Pumpkin in half, scrape out seeds and membrane. Peel each half and cut into 1/4-1/2 inch slices or cubes.
2. In a large bowl, whisk together olive oil, one clove of minced garlic, and a generous pinch of kosher salt. Add pumpkin and toss well to coat.
3. Grill pumpkin over medium to medium-high heat for a few minutes on each side or until just tender. Watch closely and don't let them burn.
4. Remove grilled pumpkin to a serving platter.

Crock-Pot Chicken & Pumpkin

Serves: 6

Ingredients:

- 2 (14.5 ounce) cans diced tomatoes
- 1 tablespoon raw honey
- 2 (14.5 ounce) cans diced tomatoes
- 2 tablespoons olive oil
- 1 onion, chopped
- 1 teaspoon ground ginger
- 1 teaspoon ground cinnamon
- 1 teaspoon ground cumin
- 1 tablespoon ground coriander

- ▸ 1½ pounds skinless, boneless chicken
- ▸ 1½ pounds skinless, boneless chicken
- ▸ breast halves, cut into bite size pieces
- ▸ 1 (15 ounce) can garbanzo beans,
- ▸ drained and rinsed
- ▸ 3 pounds fresh pumpkin, peeled and cut
- ▸ into 3/4-inch cubes
- ▸ sea salt, or to taste
- ▸ 1/4 cup water (optional)

Directions:

. Set a slow cooker to high. Place diced tomatoes and honey into the cooker; stir to combine.

. Heat olive oil in a non-stick skillet over medium-high heat. Cook onion until lightly browned, about 5 minutes.

. Mix in the ginger, cinnamon, cumin, and coriander; cook about 2 minutes. Stir in the chicken, and cook and stir until chicken is no longer pink.

Mix the garbanzo beans into the chicken mixture. Bring to a simmer.

Transfer the mixture into the slow cooker. Mix with tomatoes.

Place pumpkin into the same skillet. Reduce heat to medium.

Cook until the pumpkin is hot and some pieces are slightly browned, about 10 minutes. Stirring often.

Place pumpkin into the cooker and cover.

Cook on high setting for 1 hour. Reduce cooker setting to low, and cook until pumpkin is tender, 3 to 4 more hours. Season with sea salt and black pepper.

Funkin Facts:

Pumpkins owe their bright Orange color to the high amount of carotenoids present in them. Carotenoids assist in staving off the free radicals in the body, and help in preventing premature aging, cardiovascular diseases and other infections.

While you can use pumpkin for baking and cooking, you can certainly eat it raw to reap the nutritional benefits.

Pumpkin is a good source of potassium, a mineral that may help reduce the risk of hypertension.

Pumpkin flesh contains L-tryptophan, a chemical compound that triggers feelings of well-being and happiness.

Pumpkin is a great source of fiber, with three grams per one-cup serving and only 49 calories, it can keep you feeling full for longer on fewer calories.

Pumpkins are natural diuretics. These help in flushing out the toxins and unwanted waste material from the body - NATURALLY!

CRUSH

{ Six - Pumpkin Desserts }

"Designers want me to dress like Spring, in billowing things. I don't feel like Spring. I feel like a warm red Autumn."

~ Marilyn Monroe ~

Grain-free Chocolate chip Pumpkin Cookies

Make approx.: 12 cookies

Ingredients:

- 1 cup almond flour
- 2 tablespoons coconut flour
- 1 large egg
- 1 tablespoon coconut oil
- 3 tablespoons raw honey
- 1/4 cup pumpkin puree
- 1 teaspoon vanilla extract
- 1/8 teaspoon sea salt
- 1/4 teaspoon baking soda
- 1/4 teaspoon pumpkin spice
- 1/2 cup dark chocolate chunks

Directions:

1. Preheat oven to 350°F.
2. In a mixing bowl combine almond flour, coconut flour, baking soda, and salt.
3. Add in pumpkin puree, egg, honey, oil, and vanilla; mix well.
4. Drop tablespoons of dough on a lined baking sheet, flatten lightly.
5. Bake for 13-15 minutes.
6. Let cool and serve.

Pumpkin Facts:

The same free-radical-neutralizing powers of the carotenoids in pumpkin that may keep cancer cells at bay can also help keep the skin wrinkle-free, you get the skin-saving antioxidants from the pulp. Health magazine reported.

Easiest Soft Pumpkin & PB Cookies!

No flour! No grain!
Makes 8-10 cookies

Ingredients:

4 tablespoons peanut butter (Don't use the oily part. Use solid nut butter for these, so they do not become too moist)

1 small mashed banana (do NOT use an overly ripe banana, a new/firm banana works best)

2 tablespoons pumpkin puree

1/4 cup dark cacao chunks or use Lily's brand sweetened with stevia

1 teaspoon granulated stevia or 1 Tbsp. raw honey

Pinch of cinnamon (optional)

Directions:

. Preheat oven to 350°F.

. Combine all the ingredients.

. Scoop by rounded tablespoon onto coconut oil greased cookie sheet.

. Press down gently with fork.

. Bake in preheated 350°F oven for 12-14 minutes.

. Cookies are very soft. {and soo good!!}

The REALLY Naughty Pumpkin Cookies

30 cookies

Ingredients:

- 1 cup freshly ground oat flour
- 1/2 cup almond flour
- 2 teaspoons pumpkin pie spice
- 1/2 teaspoon sea salt
- 1/2 teaspoon baking soda
- 3/4 cup grass fed butter (room temp)
- 1 cup sucanat
- 1 large egg
- 2 teaspoons vanilla extract
- 1/2 cup pumpkin puree
- 1 cup old fashioned oats
- 1 cup dark chocolate chips

Directions:

1. Preheat oven to 375°F. Line cookie sheets with parchment paper.
2. Whisk together the flours, pumpkin pie spice, salt and baking soda.
3. In a large bowl, using a hand mixer, combine the sucanat and butter - on medium setting.
4. Add the egg, vanilla and the pumpkin. Beat for a few minutes.
5. Slowly add the flour mixture to the wet mixture and beat on low setting until a nice cookie dough forms.
6. Stir in the oats and chocolate chips.
7. Scoop out the dough in tablespoon balls, flatten slightly and place on baking sheet.
8. Bake for 13-15 minutes or until golden brown.

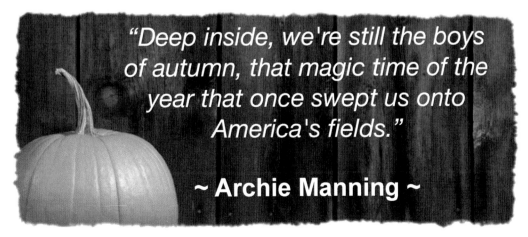

"Deep inside, we're still the boys of autumn, that magic time of the year that once swept us onto America's fields."

~ Archie Manning ~

Pumpkin Ice Cream

Servings: 8

Non-Dairy Packed with Nutrition. Less than 200 calories per serving - Including the chocolate!

Ingredients:

‣ 8 FROZEN bananas, chopped
‣ 2 cups all-natural pumpkin puree
‣ 2-4 tablespoons raw honey or pure maple syrup, depending on sweetness preferences
‣ May require 2 tablespoons unsweetened almond milk to get it blended.

Directions:

1. In your high powered blender combine the ingredients.

2. Fill a 9x13 dish with pumpkin mixture. Spread evenly. Freeze 4 hours.

Optional: Melt 1/2 cup dark chocolate/cacao, and drizzle evenly over Pumpkin Ice Cream.

3. Use scoop to serve immediately or re-freeze, tightly covered.

So Nice
I Made
It Twice!

Frozen Pumpkin Cream Pies

Makes 12 tiny treats

Ingredients:

- 1/2 tablespoon chopped hazelnuts
- 2 firm bananas
- 1 cup vanilla greek yogurt
- 1 cup pure natural pumpkin puree
- 2 tsp vanilla extract
- 1/2 teaspoon cinnamon
- 1/2 teaspoon pumpkin pie spice
- 2 teaspoon granulated stevia or 2 tablespoons raw honey

Directions:

1. Sprinkle hazelnuts lightly on the bottom of each mini cheesecake tin.
2. Blend the rest of the ingredients in blender until combined well.
3. Pour mixture into min-cheesecake tins. Freeze for 4-8 hours.
4. These should pop-out easily if you use a mini-cheesecake pan with removable / poppable bottoms.

Gooey Pumpkin Brownies

Ingredients:

- 1/3 cup coconut flour
- 1/3 cup unsweetened cocoa powder
- 1/3 cup pumpkin puree
- 1/4 cup coconut oil
- 2 teaspoons pure vanilla extract
- 4 whole eggs
- 1/2 cup pure maple syrup

Directions:

1. Whisk together the coconut flour and cocoa powder.

2. Whisk in the coconut oil, eggs, maple syrup and vanilla extract. Blend well.

3. Pour batter into a coconut-oil greased brownie pan, and bake at 350°F for about 28-35 minutes.

4. Let cool completely before removing from pan

Pumpkin Brownies to Die for!

Ingredients:

- 1 can rinsed black beans
- 1 cup Rolled Oats
- 1/2 cup unsweetened cocoa powder
- 2 tablespoons stevia
- 1/4 cup Natural Peanut Butter or Almond Butter
- 2 tablespoons coconut oil
- 2 tablespoons raw honey
- 1 tsp vanilla
- 1 scoop chocolate whey protein
- 1/2 cup unsweetened almond milk
- 1/4 teaspoon sea salt
- 1/4 cup unsweetened applesauce
- 1/4 cup pumpkin puree
- 1 teaspoon baking powder
- 1/2 teaspoon baking soda

Directions:

- Blend all ingredients in blender until you have a thick batter.
- Pour into sprayed 8x8 pan.
- Bake 350°F in pre-heated oven for approximately 40 minutes or until a toothpick comes out clean.

Pumpkin Chocolate Almond Butter

Ingredients:

- 2 cups raw almonds
- 4 tablespoons unrefined coconut oil
- 1/4 teaspoon sea salt
- 2 heaping tablespoons unsweetened cocoa powder

Directions:

1. In a food processor blend the nuts until almost butter.
2. Add the oil, the pumpkin spice, the salt and cocoa powder, and continue blending until buttery texture.
3. Store in a sealed container in the refrigerator for up to about 6 weeks.

Pumpkin Cheesecake Protein Pancakes

Delicious for Dessert!

Serves: 1

Ingredients:

- 1/3 cup rolled oats
- 1 tablespoon almond flour
- 1 scoop vanilla or chocolate whey protein
- 1/8 teaspoon baking powder
- 1/4 teaspoon pumpkin pie spice
- 1 egg white
- 1/4 cup all-natural pumpkin puree
- 2 tablespoons unsweetened almond milk

Cheesecake Ingredients:

- 3 tablespoons Vanilla Greek yogurt
- 2 tablespoons natural cottage cheese
- 1 tablespoon unsweetened almond milk
- 1 tablespoon Vanilla whey protein
- 1/2-1 teaspoon Stevia or sweetener of choice (sweetness factor is a personal preference)

Directions:

1. In a blender, process the cheesecake ingredients until smooth. Set aside.
2. In a food processor or blender, grind the oats into a fine powder.
3. Blend all pancake ingredients until smooth.
4. Heat a griddle to medium-low heat. Drop pancake batter onto griddle and cook until the top starts to bubble, then flip and cook the other side.
5. Drizzle with cheesecake topping to serve.

This coobook is filled with UNIQUE recipes including:

✓ 30+ Breakfasts
✓ 30+ Lunches
✓ 30+ Dinners
✓ 30+ Dessert and Snack ideas

Clean Food
CRUSH

Hey Ladies!

Join our Free Women's Clean Eating Community.

Includes a 5-day Clean Eating Plan & Shopping List!

There's over 7,500 members already!

Join today at: **http://CleanFoodCrush.com/challenge**

Clean Food
CRUSH

Have you downloaded your complimentary copy of

7 Days of Fun Clean Eating Recipes yet?

It's yours FREE at: **http://CleanFoodCrush.com/7days**

Thousands of copies are downloaded each month!

There are 33 Easy-to-Make Unique Recipes Inside!

Includes a Clean Eating Success Kit!

Made in the USA
Las Vegas, NV
28 February 2022